# “Shattered Silence: A Memoir of Survival of MHZ KIM”

Paperback ISBN: 978-1-304-65098-6

Hardcover ISBN: 978-1-304-65097-9

Case ID 1-13468415950

# Acknowledgments

I want to thank my four children; Lena, Jo’nee Melvin Jr., and Dominick who taught me what real love felt like my four heart beats. Last but not the least I want to thank my YouTube family, my Instagram family, Facebook family, TikTok family, who have been very supportive of this book and they can’t wait to purchase it. Thank you each and everyone and I sure you will enjoy reading it,

Thank you.

Love

MHZ Kim.

# Dedication

I would like to thank my college English Professor Mrs. Tucker, who had her students write Journals every week and I always received A's on mine, and she told me that I would make a great writer one day; that struck with me and this is my second book to have published.

I would like to thank Lena who became my mom and caretaker, if it wasn't for her, I'd have never known what it is like to forgive and not hold grudges against people who have hurt you.

# Contents

# Introduction

In the quiet corners of memory, where the echoes of a challenging past linger, there resides a story of profound resilience and unyielding strength. ""Shattered Silence: A Memoir of Survival of MHZ KIM " unveils the tumultuous yet inspiring life of Ms. Kim Smith, a remarkable individual who faced the harsh realities of an abusive childhood and turbulent relationships. This memoir transcends the confines of pain, offering a testament to the power of the human spirit to overcome adversity and emerge into the light.

As we embark on this narrative odyssey, we delve into the fragile beginnings of Ms. Smith's life, shaped by the shadows of an abusive environment. The loss of her mother at the tender age of 5 cast a long shadow, setting the stage for a journey marked by resilience and an unwavering determination to rise above circumstances.

Through the pages of this memoir, we navigate the challenges of Ms. Smith's adolescence, where the void left by her father's passing at 15 became a crucible for growth and self-discovery. The narrative unfolds as a poignant exploration of the impact of loss, the complex dynamics of relationships, and the enduring spirit that propels one forward.

"Memoir" does not merely recount the struggles; it illuminates the turning points that became beacons of hope. We witness Ms. Smith's evolution, from the echoes of abuse to the transformative moments that spurred her to break free from the cycle that threatened to define her. It is a journey through the shadows, but one that ultimately leads to the revelation of inner strength and the pursuit of healing.

This memoir is a mosaic of empowerment and advocacy, illustrating her life's commitment to inspire change and resilience in those who have faced similar challenges. As we traverse the chapters, we encounter a narrative that transcends the personal, resonating as a universal tale of triumph over trauma.

"Shattered Silence: A Memoir of Survival " is an invitation to witness the indomitable human spirit, to understand the complexities of healing, and to find hope amid the shadows. Through Ms. Smith's story, we are reminded that even in the darkest of times, there exists the potential for light, growth, and a future defined by strength and possibility. It is a story of realistic unhinged truth of the life.

# Chapter 1: Fragile Beginnings

Life, if you see it as a person is very difficult with a lot of concerns, distress, and trenches. But if you feel life, it is the most exquisite gift to all human kind. Having said that, we all were sent to the earth as a punishment yet god did give us all the immunity to live our lives with courses our own accord; religion, believes, creed, caste, etc. My story prevails the journey of my faith, finding hope in the darkest of the moments, being grateful to the Almighty in the abys of chaos. I have been through a lot; physically, mental, and emotionally. Abuse makes us naïve, thoughtless, and emotionally bound to depend. Although, we can get the help and heal ourselves. But in order to do so we all have to keep the traumas in line; face to face, so that we would be able to move on.

My life, akin to a complex tapestry woven with threads of joy and sorrow, unfolds in ways unpredictable and profound. I find solace in viewing life not as an adversary but as a gift bestowed upon humanity. My personal odyssey echoes the poignant struggles that test the resilience of the human spirit.

My journey commences against a backdrop of adversity, where the hues of distress and trenches paint the canvas of my early years. Sent to Earth, as I contemplate, almost as a form of divine retribution, I grapple with the paradox of existence. Nevertheless, amid the chaos, a profound realization emerges — the immunity granted by the Almighty to traverse life's varied courses, shaped by religious, cultural, and personal beliefs.

In the depths of my narrative, I reveal the crucible of my faith, the beacon that guides me through the darkest moments. Gratitude becomes my armor in the abyss of chaos, a testament to my unwavering connection with the divine. The echoes of my story resonate with the unyielding pursuit of hope, an elusive companion that I seek amidst life's tumultuous currents.

The shadows of my past extend beyond mere philosophical musings; they are etched in the fabric of my experiences. Physical, mental, and emotional tribulations mark the waypoints on my arduous path. Abuse, a formidable adversary, leaves an indelible imprint, rendering the innocent naïve, thoughtless, and emotionally shackled.

Yet, within the heart of despair, I find resilience. I acknowledge the transformative power of seeking help, of healing wounds both seen and unseen. My incidents unfold against the backdrop of a profound loss, as my parents departed from my life prematurely. My mother, a guardian and protector, succumbed when I was but a five-year-old, leaving me to grapple with the incomprehensible reality of loss. I lost both of my parents at a very young age; my mom, when I was five-year-old and my dad when I was fifteen year old. My father was in the Army and had a drinking problem. He also suffered from epilepsy which I got to know later in life, as my mother was always there to help him out. When my mother died, my father came to me and told me that my mother has passed away. I was too young to comprehend what he told me. As stated, before, my father had drinking addiction, so he wasn't able to take care of me and my siblings. As the time prevails everything, the sadness over took us all the siblings, even though, I didn't understand much but the void of her absences made it very difficult for me to not to feel anything. Admits of everything; my eldest sister, called Lena. She was our mother's best friend. My elder sister was just looking out her younger siblings, she didn't know what would Lena actually do to us. Lena's presence made it very difficult of us all to live; we all were just kids and trying to survive the hostile situation. Although, mu sister had the best intentions at her heart when she called Lena for the help. Little did she know that Lena would be tormenting us the rest of the life. The torture was so terrifying and traumatizing that we never felt the love or warmth.

My father, a soldier with battles both internal and external, struggled with a drinking problem and the hidden burden of epilepsy. The revelation of his affliction, hidden beneath the veneer of military duty, unveiled itself only after my mother's demise. Left orphaned and vulnerable, I faced the harsh realities of a fractured family.

In the absence of parental guidance, my father's struggles with addiction left a void that Lena, my mother's best friend, endeavored to fill. However, the purported sanctuary of care transformed into a crucible of torment as Lena, the caretaker, became the architect of our suffering. Abuse, insidious and shrouded in darkness, bound me and my siblings in a web of anguish.

The opening chapter of my life story unfolds with delicate strokes, capturing the fragility of beginnings marred by loss and abuse. As the tapestry of my narrative unravels, you are invited into a realm where faith, hope, and resilience become the guiding stars in the night sky of adversity.

Left orphaned and vulnerable, the once-sturdy pillars of family crumble, exposing the raw edges of my fractured reality. In the absence of parental guidance, my father's struggles with addiction cast long shadows, leaving an indelible void that Lena, my mother's best friend, attempts to fill.

Amidst the pain, the canvas of my early years is painted with strokes of resilience, a silent testimony to the transformative power of seeking help. The delicate intricacies of my journey invite you into a realm where faith, hope, and resilience emerge as guiding stars, piercing through the night sky of adversity. The story of my life is etched with the profound realization that, even in the face of darkness, there exists a possibility for healing and redemption.

My life took a sudden shift, not in my early years as I was too little to understand what had truly occurred, but when I did, it drenched my heart and soul in a way that I was never able to recover from. The sole caregiver my siblings and I had during all of this suffering was abusive. My life became even more terrible as a result of these events.

In the tender recesses of my five-year-old heart, losing my mother felt like a storm that had unexpectedly swept away all the familiar warmth and safety. The news, delivered by my father with a heavy heart, was a puzzle my young mind struggled to piece together. It left me standing on the edge of an emotional precipice, my little world suddenly tilted and uncertain.

Confusion reigned as I grappled with the void left by her absence. Her laughter, the comforting touch of her hand, and the lullabies that once filled our home were replaced by a deafening silence. At first, I couldn't quite fathom the permanence of her departure. I found myself waiting by the door, hoping she'd return, her embrace dispelling the shadows that crept into my world.

As days turned into weeks, the reality of her absence began to settle in, and an ache, both sharp and persistent, lodged itself in my chest. I became acutely aware of the emptiness at the dinner table, the untouched toys that once brought joy in her presence. Each night, I would clasp my hands in prayer, sending whispered messages to the heavens, hoping she could hear my yearning for just one more moment with her.

The world, once a playground of joy and wonder, now wore a somber hue. I felt like a fragile leaf caught in the relentless currents of grief, swirling through a world that had lost its familiar colors. The simplest tasks became arduous as I navigated the confusing landscape of emotions – a kaleidoscope of sadness, anger, and an inexplicable longing for the familiar contours of my mother's love.

In the quiet moments of solitude, I would trace the lines of her photograph, my small fingers grazing the image that held the essence of what was now a distant memory. Night after night, I found solace in the tears that flowed, a river carrying the weight of my grief. The nights became an intimate dialogue with the stars, as I whispered my hopes and fears to the celestial canvas, hoping that somewhere, somehow, my mother could hear.

The absence of her presence was a puzzle I couldn't solve, a riddle that left my young heart heavy with an emotion too profound for my tender age. In the midst of it all, I clung to the remnants of her love, an ethereal thread that connected me to a world forever altered by loss.

## Chapter 02: Fragments of Silence

In the hushed corridors of my once lively home, echoes of my mother's laughter lingered like fragile whispers in the wind. But now, a shroud of melancholy draped over the rooms, casting shadows that seemed to devour the remnants of joy that once resided within these walls.

Since my mother's departure, a chilling silence had settled, broken only by the creaks and groans of a house bearing the weight of sorrow. In her absence, a caregiver named Lena had taken us to her residence, to provide us a proper place to live.. Her eyes held a hardness that seemed to penetrate through the very soul, and her footsteps echoed with an unspoken menace.

My father, a mere shell of the man he once was, had succumbed to the numbing embrace of alcohol. The bottles, like silent witnesses, lined the shelves—a testament to his silent battle, a futile attempt to drown the pain of losing the love of his life. He, too, was a casualty in the war waged against our family.

With my mother gone and my father incapacitated by his own demons, the responsibility of nurturing fell onto Lena's shoulders. But nurturing was a word foreign to her, a concept lost in the cold gaze she cast upon us, my siblings and me. Her hands, once meant for care, now felt like shackles, chaining us to a reality too harsh for young shoulders to bear.

The house, once vibrant, now exuded an air of desolation. Darkened corners seemed to harbor secrets, and the walls absorbed the stifled cries of my siblings. We lived in a silence punctuated only by the sharpness of Lena's commands, each word cutting through the air like a whip.

I found solace in my mother's belongings, the fragments of her life that lingered in the forgotten corners of our home. A worn-out scarf, a faded photograph—each piece was a lifeline to a past that felt increasingly elusive. In the stillness of my room, I clung to these relics, desperate to preserve the essence of a love that had been snatched away too soon.

The nights were the hardest. The darkness became a canvas on which my fears painted grotesque images. Lena's footsteps, ominous and foreboding, haunted the hallways. Her voice, devoid of kindness, became a symphony of cruelty that reverberated through the emptiness of our home.

My siblings, innocent souls navigating a world tilted off its axis, bore the brunt of Lena's malevolence. In their tearful eyes, I saw the reflection of my own helplessness. We were prisoners in our own home, captives of circumstance, yearning for a reprieve that never came.

As the days blurred into a monotonous parade of sorrow, I clung to the flickering hope that somewhere, amidst the ruins of our family, a glimmer of light would pierce through the darkness. Little did I know, the journey toward that light would demand a resilience I never knew I possessed—a strength forged in the crucible of adversity, fueled by the enduring love of a mother who, though gone, remained a beacon in the recesses of my heart.

As the hands of time continued their relentless march, I found myself navigating the treacherous terrain of adolescence under the oppressive weight of Lena's care—or rather, her version of it. I was young and vulnerable, a fragile soul tethered to the whims of an abusive caretaker who seemed to revel in her power.

The once vibrant hues of my childhood had faded into a palette of muted grays, each day a struggle against the encroaching darkness that seemed to seep into every crevice of our sanctuary. Lena's influence extended beyond the physical realm; it was a toxic mist that clouded my thoughts and stunted my growth. Her words, like venom, poisoned the fertile ground of my young mind, leaving scars that ran deeper than any physical wounds.

I became a ghost in my own life, a shadow that flitted through the hallways, tiptoeing around the volatile atmosphere that clung to our home like a malevolent specter. My once sparkling eyes were now windows to a soul wearied by the ceaseless battle for survival. I longed for the warmth of a mother's embrace, the tender reassurance that life could be kind, even in the absence of perfection.

Lena's cruelty manifested in myriad ways. A harsh word here, a dismissive glance there—the arsenal of her torment was vast and unrelenting. The scars on my skin were eclipsed by the invisible wounds etched into my psyche, wounds that festered in the silence I was forced to inhabit.

My vulnerability became a weapon in her hands, a tool she wielded with precision to assert dominance. The very essence of childhood, a time meant for innocence and exploration, was replaced by a constant state of vigilance. I learned to navigate the unpredictable currents of Lena's moods, tiptoeing around the minefield of her displeasure, desperate to avoid the explosions that followed.

In the confines of our stifling home, my siblings and I became each other's silent allies. We communicated in stolen glances, a language born out of necessity, a means to share the burden of our collective suffering. Their faces mirrored my own struggles, etched with a premature understanding of a world that had robbed us of our naivety.

As the seasons changed outside our windows, I yearned for change within the walls that held us captive. The ache for a reprieve, a semblance of normalcy, intensified with each passing day. Yet, the specter of Lena loomed large, an indomitable force that crushed the fragile buds of hope before they could bloom.

In the solitude of my room, I clung to the memories of my mother like a lifeline. Her gentle touch, the lullabies that once cradled me to sleep—they became the armor that shielded my spirit from complete dissolution. In the midst of the darkness, I found solace in the fragments of her love that lingered, resilient against the corrosive forces at play.

Little did I know that the storm within would eventually propel me toward a journey of self-discovery—a journey that would test the limits of my resilience and unveil the dormant strength that had lain dormant within my young heart.

# Chapter 03: Shattered, tormented, and broken…

I woke up that morning with a pit in my stomach, knowing it was another day of navigating the unpredictable waves of Lena's temper. The incident at school had left me with a sense of dread that clung to me like a heavy fog.

As I walked through the front door, Lena's stern gaze met mine. Her eyes, normally cold, seemed to burn with a fiery anger that sent shivers down my spine. I knew something bad was about to happen; I just didn't know what.

Lena's voice, sharp and unforgiving, demanded an explanation for the lost item. Fear tightened my chest as I stammered through the story, but it wasn't enough. Her anger boiled over, and suddenly, I found myself at the mercy of the extension cord.

The first strike felt like a surge of electricity, the pain coursing through me in waves. Each subsequent lash left a physical mark on my skin and a deeper wound in my soul. Tears welled in my eyes, a mixture of pain and a profound sense of betrayal.

The cord left angry welts on my back, a painful reminder of the abuse I endured at the hands of the person who was supposed to care for me. As Lena's rage subsided, I curled into myself, aching both physically and emotionally.

In that moment, I felt a profound sense of isolation. The world outside seemed oblivious to the torment within these walls. The weight of shame and humiliation pressed down on me, and I struggled to make sense of the injustice I had just experienced.

Lena's actions had torn away a piece of my innocence, replaced with a growing sense of vulnerability and mistrust. Each day became a battle between survival and surrender, a relentless struggle that left me longing for a glimmer of hope to break through the darkness.

My father, once a pillar of strength, had crumbled beneath the weight of his grief. The loss of my mother had left him hollow, a mere shell of the man he used to be. His eyes, once filled with warmth, now held a vacant stare that seemed to gaze into a past that haunted him.

As Lena's abuse continued, I saw the toll it took on my father. He became a silent spectator to my suffering, unable to summon the strength to intervene. His attempts to shield himself from the pain had left him emotionally detached, a prisoner of his own despair.

I could sense the internal struggle within him, a battle between the love for his family and the overwhelming grief that paralyzed him. The house echoed with the silence of unspoken words and unshed tears, creating a suffocating atmosphere that weighed heavily on my shoulders.

There were moments when he would catch my eye, his expression a mixture of guilt and powerlessness. It was as if he wanted to reach out, to shield me from the storm, but the tempest within him was too fierce.

The emotional chasm widened with each passing day, pushing us further apart. The man who once comforted me with bedtime stories and gentle lullabies had become a mere phantom in our home, haunted by memories and unable to rescue us from the nightmare that unfolded.

In my heart, I held onto the hope that someday he would break free from the chains of grief, that he would find the strength to be the father we so desperately needed. But as the days turned into weeks, and the weeks into months, that hope flickered like a dying flame, leaving me in the cold shadows of a broken family.

# Chapter 04: Liberation

The day I left that oppressive home marked the beginning of my journey toward liberation. At the age of 20, I carried the weight of scars etched into my skin and soul, remnants of a tumultuous upbringing. Lena's unwarranted accusations, branding me a slut, echoed in my ears, but I was determined to break free from the shackles of her twisted narrative.

As I stepped out into the world, I found refuge in the arms of a boyfriend who saw me for who I truly was—a survivor, not a victim. Together, we embarked on a shared odyssey, navigating the complexities of healing and self-discovery.

Leaving that little hell behind was both terrifying and exhilarating. The wounds of the past were still fresh, but the promise of a new beginning fueled my courage. My father, trapped in his own emotional turmoil, remained behind, a silent figure in the rearview mirror as my boyfriend and I drove away.

The transition to a life of my own came with challenges. Lena's toxic words lingered in my mind, threatening to undermine the newfound strength I was cultivating. Yet, surrounded by the support of a loving partner, I began shedding the layers of self-doubt she had imposed upon me.

Our shared home became a sanctuary, a place where I could rebuild and redefine myself. In the tenderness of my boyfriend's love, I discovered the healing power of genuine connection. Together, we faced the demons of my past, dismantling the false narrative that had haunted me for far too long.

Leaving that abusive environment wasn't just a physical escape; it was a declaration of autonomy and self-love. The scars would forever bear witness to the battles fought, but they no longer defined me. With every step away from the shadows of my past, I embraced the freedom to live a life of my own choosing, liberated from the chains that once bound me.

# Chapter 05: Echoes of Silence

The walls of our once vibrant home, guardians of laughter and warmth, now seemed to close in on me like an oppressive embrace. I was no stranger to the shadows that lingered in every corner, silent witnesses to the unraveling of our family. As a teenager, the weight of my father's grief pressed upon my shoulders, threatening to crush the remnants of our shattered joy.

The air hung heavy with the stifling silence that accompanied his grieving presence. The creaking floorboards beneath his weight echoed the somber steps of a man consumed by sorrow, and my heart quickened in sync with the approaching melancholy. The once familiar sound of his laughter now carried the weight of a grieving melody, foretelling the impending storm of his heartache.

In those moments, I found solace in the sanctuary of my thoughts. The internal dialogue became a lifeline, a fragile thread connecting me to the reality we yearned to escape. I traced the contours of my memories, desperately holding onto the fragments of a time when love was untainted, and our family was whole.

The sorrow manifested in subtle ways, leaving scars that ran deeper than the visible bruises. His words, laced with the bitterness of loss, became a relentless assault on our collective spirits. As a teenager navigating the turbulent waters of adolescence, each sorrowful remark became a chisel, carving away at the foundation of our shared identity.

I became a silent observer of our own life, an unwilling participant in a twisted theatre of pain. The fear of his unpredictable sorrow loomed like a storm cloud, casting a perpetual shadow over our existence. The once vibrant colors of my teenage years faded into a monochrome existence, devoid of the joy and spontaneity that should have defined this chapter of my life.

I gazed into the mirror, searching for traces of the girl I used to be. The reflection that stared back at me was a stranger, eyes haunted by the grief inflicted by the one who was supposed to be our protector. The girl in the mirror was a prisoner, her spirit confined to the labyrinth of sorrow and uncertainty.

The nights were the worst, each passing hour a cruel reminder of the darkness that enveloped our home. Sleep became an elusive companion, chased away by the nightmares that played out in the theater of my mind. I longed for the morning light to banish the shadows, if only temporarily.

Yet, within the cocoon of despair, a flicker of defiance ignited. A whisper of resilience urged me to endure, to cling to the hope that one day the echoes of silence would be replaced by the symphony of healing. As a teenager trapped in this nightmare, I nurtured a silent rebellion, an uprising of the spirit against the oppression that sought to snuff out our light.

In the crucible of adversity, I discovered an unspoken strength that defied the constraints of our circumstances. The tears that fell in the solitude of my room were not signs of weakness but tributes to the indomitable will that refused to be extinguished. As I weathered the storm of sorrow, I held onto the belief that, one day, the echoes of silence would be drowned out by the triumphant roar of our collective healing. As the final echoes of that tumultuous phase faded away, a newfound sense of freedom embraced us. We were survivors, not just of the storms that had ravaged our home but also of the emotional tempests that had threatened to engulf our spirits. The resilience that had blossomed within the crucible of adversity now stood as a testament to the unwavering strength of the human spirit.

With the closing of that chapter, we stepped into the uncharted territory of a future untethered by the shackles of abuse. The journey toward healing was ongoing, but with each sunrise, we embraced the promise of renewal. The fragments of my shattered innocence, though forever altered, became the foundation upon which I built a life defined by resilience, strength, and the unwavering belief that, in the face of darkness, the light within us can prevail.

## Chapter 06: Dance of Despair

The air in the house felt different after the storm of revelation. As the youngest sibling, I found myself caught in the delicate dance between the remnants of despair and the fragile promise of change. It was a strange symphony of emotions, a cacophony of hope and uncertainty that played out in every corner of our once-turbulent home.

Each step I took was laden with the weight of newfound responsibility. The protective instinct, long dormant, surged within me, driving me to shield my siblings from the lingering shadows that still clung to our shared history. The dance became a tightrope act, a balancing act between nurturing their sense of security and confronting the ghosts that lingered in the recesses of our past.

At school, sympathetic glances and hushed whispers followed our every move. The camaraderie of teachers and classmates became a bittersweet reassurance that we were no longer prisoners of our secret. Yet, the hallways still echoed with judgment, a reminder that the scars of our past were not easily erased.

Evenings, once taut with tension, gradually transformed into moments of tentative normalcy. The dinner table, once a battleground, became a space for tentative conversations and shared laughter. The wounds on our hearts, though not forgotten, served as markers of the strength that had emerged from the crucible of our shared adversity.

In the sanctuary of my room, I grappled with conflicting emotions. The healing process felt like navigating a maze of forgiveness and acceptance. As a teenager, the dance of despair unfolded within the confines of my own soul, a struggle to reconcile the love I once held with the wounds that still festered.

Restless dreams haunted my nights, vivid reminders of our collective past. The dance continued even in sleep, where the specters of our shared trauma manifested as phantoms that twirled at the edges of consciousness. Yet, within the darkness of the night, a glimmer of hope persisted—a reminder that the dance of despair could evolve into a ballet of resilience.

Days turned into weeks, and weeks into months, marking the rhythm of our gradual transformation. The wounds, though not erased, began to heal, and the scars became symbols of survival rather than sources of pain. The house, once haunted by the echoes of despair, now resonated with the tentative notes of recovery.

In the intricate choreography of our shared existence, the dance of despair played a pivotal role—a bridge between the shadows of the past and the promise of a brighter future. As a teenager entangled in this delicate dance, I embraced the complexity of emotions, knowing that the steps toward healing were as unique as the individuals taking them. The music of change played on, and with each carefully measured step, we moved closer to a harmonious resolution, where the echoes of despair would be replaced by the symphony of renewal.

The days that followed the revelation unfolded with a delicate unpredictability. The atmosphere at home, though less oppressive, retained a residue of the storm that had passed through. We, the siblings, navigated the uncharted territory of this new normal, our shared glances revealing a silent understanding of the journey that lay ahead.

Embracing my position as the youngest sibling, I discovered a unique role that became a steadfast companion—a blend of responsibility that both weighed on me and granted me strength. Within the confines of our home, a subtle dance unfolded, intertwining moments of healing with threads of remembrance. I frequently found myself navigating the delicate balance of being a protector of their delicate tranquility and an active participant in our shared journey toward liberation.

At school, the sympathetic glances evolved into subtle nods of encouragement. Teachers became allies in our battle against the stigma that clung to us like a persistent shadow. Yet, the judgmental whispers persisted, reminders that the scars we carried were not easily concealed. The hallways remained a battlefield of perception, and each step became a declaration of resilience.

Evenings brought a semblance of routine, a tentative return to the mundane activities that had once defined our family life. The dinner table conversations wavered between cautious optimism and the unspoken acknowledgment of our shared wounds. Laughter, though hesitant, began to punctuate the air, pushing against the lingering echoes of despair.

In the stillness of my room, I grappled with my own internal dance. The wounds on my soul, once raw and exposed, began to scab over. Forgiveness and acceptance became elusive partners, swirling around me like distant dancers in a ballroom of emotions. I knew that my father was going through a tough time, so I never actually said anything to him. I knew damn well, how it feels to lose a loved one, and he only had my mother, so I forgave him with my heart.

Nights carried the weight of restless dreams, vivid narratives woven with threads of our collective history. The dance continued, even in the sanctuary of sleep, as phantoms of the past twirled in the shadows of my subconscious. Yet, within those nocturnal struggles, a seed of hope sprouted—an unwavering belief that the dance of despair could be transformed into a dance of resilience.

As the weeks unfolded, a subtle metamorphosis began to take shape. The wounds, though not forgotten, no longer dictated the rhythm of our lives. The house, once a battlefield, started to echo with tentative notes of recovery. The dance of despair, once chaotic and discordant, evolved into a choreography of healing.

The resilience we discovered within ourselves became a guiding force. Each step we took, whether in the hallowed halls of our school or the familiar corridors of our home, became a testament to our collective strength. The dance of despair, though not erased, no longer held us captive; instead, it propelled us forward into a future where the echoes of our past would serve as a backdrop to the symphony of our renewal.

In the intricate choreography of our shared existence, continued to unfold—a chapter marked not only by the dance of despair but by the gradual emergence of a resilient spirit, determined to reclaim the fragments of our shattered innocence. The music of change played on, and as we embraced the transformative dance, the promise of a brighter future beckoned on the horizon.

In the wake of revelation, the fragile threads of transformation continued to weave through the fabric of our lives. The palpable shift in the atmosphere at home, though subtle, bore the promise of a gradual healing. As the youngest sibling, my role became that of a guide through the labyrinth of emotions that defined our newfound reality.

The dance of despair persisted, albeit with a gentler sway. Each day presented a new set of challenges and triumphs, as we navigated the uncharted waters of healing. The weight of responsibility, both as a protector and participant in our shared struggle, became a constant reminder of the delicate balance we sought to maintain.

School, once a battlefield of judgment, transformed into a haven of understanding. The sympathetic glances evolved into genuine support, and teachers emerged as advocates for our journey toward normalization. Yet, the lingering whispers in the hallways served as a stark reminder that the judgments of others were not easily shaken off. The dance with perception continued, a complex choreography of resilience and vulnerability.

Evenings at home underwent a metamorphosis, becoming a canvas for the tentative strokes of normalcy. The dinner table, once a place of tension, transformed into a space where laughter and conversation found their way back. The wounds we shared became bridges rather than barriers, connecting us in our collective pursuit of healing.

In the quietude of my room, I grappled with the internal dance of conflicting emotions. The scars on my soul, though healing, still pulsed with the echoes of the past. Forgiveness, a nebulous concept, remained elusive, and acceptance became a journey rather than a destination. The dance of despair played out within the recesses of my thoughts, a reflection of the intricate tapestry of emotions that defined my teenage years.

Nights held a different tenor—a nuanced symphony of dreams that bore the imprints of our collective history. The dance persisted, even in the sanctuary of sleep, as phantoms twirled in the shadows of my subconscious. Yet, within those nocturnal struggles, a seed of hope sprouted—an unwavering belief that the dance of despair could evolve into a dance of resilience.

Weeks turned into months, and the subtle transformation continued its course. The wounds, though still visible, no longer dictated the narrative of our lives. The house, once fraught with tension, resonated with notes of recovery. The dance of despair, once a tumultuous whirlwind, began to resemble a more graceful waltz, a testament to the resilience that unfolded within our collective spirit.

The resilience that blossomed within us became a beacon of light, guiding us through the intricate choreography of healing. Each step forward, whether within the familiar corridors of home or the hallways of school, marked a triumph over the echoes of our painful history. The dance of despair, though not forgotten, no longer held us captive; instead, it propelled us toward a future where the scars of our past became badges of strength.

The promise of a brighter future beckoned, and with each carefully measured step, we embraced the transformative dance that would lead us further away from despair and into the harmonious embrace of renewal.

## Chapter 07: The Weight of Loss

I never imagined life without Dad. His booming laugh and the warmth of his hugs were constants, a sanctuary I thought would always be there. But then, everything changed. My dad's heart gave out, he was admitted to the hospital and was going through all the medical care. But unfortunately, he went into comma and never came back to us. We all were left alone in this miserable world by ourselves. As all of my siblings had their life settled, I was the youngest one, thus I had to live with Lena even after my dad died. The torment went up in the levels when he left this world. She got more abusive than ever.

Now that, all my siblings had their lives, I was the only one left with Lena. Her ways of living made it more difficult for me to survive in the house that I could never call my home, though I have forgiven her for the things that she did and yet I cannot shake the turmoil that I once felt in her presence. Her strict rules and constant monitoring made home feel less like a refuge and more like a prison.

Debra, my sister, retreated into her books, seeking solace between the pages to escape the chaos that now dominated our once harmonious household.

As for me, I struggled to accept this new arrangement. Lena's attempts at structure felt like an intrusion into the little control I still had. Her gaze, filled with judgment, weighed heavily on my every move. She tried to impose routines, enforce meal times, and dictate our chores, as if grief could be managed by following a schedule.

Every day was a battle between honoring Dad's memory and facing the harsh reality of our altered lives. Memories of him flooded my thoughts at unexpected moments, like a tidal wave threatening to drown me in sorrow. I missed the way he'd listen to my worries and offer advice, the way his presence brought a sense of calmness to our home.

Living under Lena's watchful eye felt like being boxed in, trapped in a life that didn't belong to us anymore. I yearned for the freedom to grieve in my own way, without someone hovering over my shoulder, telling me how to feel or what to do.

I knew Lena meant well, but her overbearing nature intensified our pain. I wanted to scream at her, to make her understand that no amount of rules or structure could mend our shattered hearts. But instead, I swallowed my anger and retreated to the solitude of my room, seeking solace in the darkness that mirrored the heaviness in my heart.

In those quiet moments, I found myself grappling with a whirlwind of emotions—grief, anger, and an overwhelming sense of helplessness. I wondered if life would ever feel normal again, or if this new normal was something we'd have to accept, whether we wanted to or not.

As I lay on my bed, staring at the ceiling, I whispered to the emptiness around me, longing for the comfort of Dad's presence. The ache of loss gnawed at my soul, and I found myself wishing for a way to escape this unbearable reality.

But amidst the chaos of emotions, a glimmer of hope flickered—a reminder that maybe, just maybe, we could find a way to heal, even in the midst of Lena's suffocating presence. I clung to that tiny spark, holding onto the belief that somehow, someday, we would emerge from this darkness stronger, together.

Days turned into weeks, and the suffocating weight of grief lingered like an uninvited guest in our home. Lena's attempts to enforce routine felt like a constant tug-of-war between her authority and our desire for freedom amidst our mourning.

Each morning felt like an uphill battle. I struggled to get out of bed, wrestling with the memories that haunted my dreams. The aroma of breakfast wafted through the house, a stark contrast to the heaviness that hung in the air. Lena's well-intentioned gestures felt like a mockery of our pain. She would smile and say things like, "Time heals all wounds," as if her clichéd wisdom could magically mend our shattered hearts.

At times, I found myself retreating into the sanctuary of Dad's old study, surrounded by the familiar scent of his books and the comforting embrace of memories. His absence felt more profound in the spaces he used to occupy, the silence echoing the void he left behind.

Lena's attempts at bonding felt forced, her questions probing into our emotions like a surgeon's scalpel, dissecting our grief. I longed for someone to understand that grief isn't something that can be neatly compartmentalized or explained away. It's a raw, jagged edge that cuts through the fabric of our lives, leaving us bleeding and vulnerable.

As the days melded into an unending cycle of monotony, I found solace in the simplest of things—a stray beam of sunlight filtering through the window, the gentle rustle of leaves outside, or the way my sister's eyes would briefly light up when she lost herself in a particularly captivating story.

One evening, while sitting in the garden, the sun dipping below the horizon, I found Lena standing by the fading roses, lost in her own thoughts. For a moment, the hard lines of her face softened, and I glimpsed a vulnerability that mirrored our own. It was in that fleeting moment that I realized perhaps she too was grappling with her own form of loss, trying to navigate a path in this intricate labyrinth of grief. Despite the friction between us, I sensed a shared ache—the ache of missing someone dear, the ache of feeling inadequate in the face of overwhelming emotions.

I swallowed the bitterness that had consumed me and tentatively approached her. "I miss him too," I murmured softly, surprising even myself with the vulnerability in my own voice.

Her eyes, glistening with unshed tears, met mine. In that instant, the wall between us crumbled, and for the first time, I saw her not just as an intruder in our lives, but as someone who also carried the weight of sorrow.

In that fragile moment of understanding, a flicker of empathy ignited—a tiny ember amidst the darkness. Maybe, just maybe, we could find a way to navigate this tumultuous journey together, leaning on each other for support rather than pushing against the tide of grief.

As the night descended, enveloping us in a blanket of stars, I allowed myself a sliver of hope—a whisper that maybe, in the shared pain, we could find a path toward healing, slowly inching our way out of the suffocating grasp of grief.

# Chapter 08: Embracing My Own Path

Life felt like a delicate balancing act, constantly juggling the needs of my family against the longing to reclaim a semblance of my own identity. The weight of responsibility hung heavy on my shoulders, woven with the threads of duty, sacrifice, and the ever-lingering ache of loss.

Amidst the chaos, I sought solace in the gentle whispers of the wind and the quiet moments stolen in the early hours before the world awoke. My siblings, though still grappling with their own grief, leaned on me as a pillar of strength, blurring the lines between sister and parental figure.

And then there was Melvin Sr.., my boyfriend—or perhaps, I should say, my ex-husband now. The fractures in our relationship began to surface like hairline cracks, barely noticeable at first. His infidelity shattered the fragile trust I had painstakingly built, leaving behind shards of broken promises and shattered dreams.

Melvin - his name alone conjures a kaleidoscope of emotions within me. In the labyrinth of my teenage years, he emerged as a steadfast companion, a source of solace amid the tumult of my reality. This chapter unfurls the tapestry of our connection, a testament to the unexpected joys that blossomed in the midst of despair.

From the moment our worlds collided, Melvin proved to be a beacon of light in the shadows. His presence, like a gentle breeze in a storm, brought a sense of calm that I desperately craved. With eyes that held an ocean of understanding, he navigated the complexities of my emotions with an empathy that transcended the spoken word.

Melvin wasn't just a boyfriend; he was a confidant, a sanctuary where I could unravel the layers of my pain without fear of judgment. His laughter became the melody that accompanied the dance of our shared moments, a harmonious counterpoint to the dissonance that echoed in the recesses of my family life.

Our connection wasn't born out of the need to escape reality but rather a mutual desire to create a refuge within it. In the quiet corners of our conversations, he became a co-author of my healing narrative, a collaborator in the dance of resilience that unfolded within me. His love was a balm for the wounds that lingered, and his unwavering support became a cornerstone of my strength.

Melvin's world was one of enchantment—a realm where love and understanding reigned supreme. In his embrace, the echoes of despair faded into the background, drowned out by the symphony of affection that enveloped us. He wasn't just a lover; he was a guardian of my fragile peace, a knight who stood beside me in the battles I fought within myself.

The tender moments we shared became lighthouses, guiding me through the storms that raged around me. His touch, a gentle caress, spoke volumes of a love that transcended the scars of my past. In his eyes, I found a reflection of the strength I had forgotten existed within me, a reminder that love could be a catalyst for healing.

As a teenager traversing the landscape of abuse, Melvin's unwavering presence became a lifeline. The understanding between us wasn't born from shared experiences of pain but rather a shared commitment to healing. Together, we navigated the intricate dance between despair and hope, forging a connection that withstood the tests of our tumultuous reality.

The chapters of my life with Melvin unfolded like a love story etched in resilience. He wasn't a savior, for the power to heal lay within me, but he became a co-pilot in the journey toward redemption. In his arms, I discovered that love could be an anchor in the storm, a force that could defy the echoes of despair and propel us toward the promise of renewal.

As this unfolds, Melvin remains a pivotal character—a guardian of my heart, a witness to my struggles, and a partner in the transformative dance of resilience. The whispers of Melvin linger in the pages of my life, a love story woven into the fabric of my teenage years, reminding me that even in the midst of darkness, love can be a powerful force that illuminates the path toward healing.

I found myself picking up the pieces, not just of my own heart, but also of his children—children he kept leaving in my care as he chased temporary gratification elsewhere. I tried to shield my children from the turmoil, but the strain began to show in the furrowed lines etched on my brow and the weariness that seeped into my bones.

The children, innocent souls caught in the crossfire of their parents' choices, looked at me with eyes that mirrored confusion and yearning for stability. I couldn't turn them away, even as their presence added weight to the already burdensome load I carried.

As I navigated the delicate dance between caretaker and guardian, I felt the tug-of-war between my innate desire to nurture and the longing to reclaim my own life. Days blurred together—a whirlwind of responsibilities, sleepless nights, and heartache that left me teetering on the edge of exhaustion.

In the midst of this turmoil, I realized that I had lost sight of myself. The once-vibrant dreams and aspirations had faded into the background, obscured by the fog of obligations. I yearned for the freedom to pursue my own passions, to carve a path that was uniquely mine.

The realization was a catalyst—a gentle awakening within me. I began to take tentative steps toward reclaiming my identity, rediscovering the hobbies and interests that had once brought joy to my life. I sought solace in writing, pouring the tumultuous whirlwind of emotions onto the blank pages, finding a semblance of peace in the cathartic release of words.

With each sunrise, I found the strength to redefine the boundaries of my existence, to nurture not just the needs of my family but also the neglected corners of my soul. It was a slow and arduous journey, a delicate balance between duty and self-discovery.

And amidst the chaos and struggles, a tiny seed of hope sprouted within me—a belief that I could rewrite my story, weaving resilience and determination into the tapestry of my life. I learned to set boundaries, to say no to the burdens that weren't mine to carry, and to embrace the freedom that came with reclaiming my autonomy.

As I stood on the precipice of uncertainty, gazing at the horizon painted with hues of possibility, I knew that the road ahead would be fraught with challenges. But armed with newfound strength and a renewed sense of self-worth, I embraced the journey, ready to carve a path that belonged solely to me.

# Chapter: 9 Crossroads of Destiny

We all fall in love when we are young, and life extends a gracious hand, inviting us to savor the carefree days. For me, this sentiment was a reality woven into every fiber of my being during the time spent with Melvin. He wasn't just a love; he was my sanctuary, a sturdy pillar in the tempest of life.

The decision to be with Melvin, however, was not without its challenges. Lena, vehemently opposed the idea of me stepping into a life entwined with Melvin's. Yet, when the chance presented itself, I seized it, eloping with the man who held my heart. Our journey together was marked by joy, laughter, and the promise of a future entwined with each other.

Melvin, having been a parent before, approached our newfound parenthood with a profound sense of responsibility and love. He was not just a provider but a guardian, a guide, and a beacon of support. Our children became the living testament to our union, and Melvin, despite prior experiences, embraced fatherhood anew with unwavering enthusiasm.

However, the tapestry of our love wasn't without its frayed edges. Loyalty, a delicate thread in the fabric of relationships, sometimes proved brittle. Yet, I harbored no resentment; when fidelity faltered, we navigated the currents of life and parted ways amicably. Life, I realized, has an uncanny knack for guiding our energies where they are meant to be.

In the narrative of love, our tale reached a critical juncture, a crossroads of destiny where choices were made, and consequences unfolded. This chapter in our shared history explored the transient nature of loyalty and the unpredictable paths life lays before us. As the pages turned, the echoes of our past decisions resonated, shaping the contours of the future that lay ahead, promising both heartache and redemption.

The crossroads of destiny stood before us, a pivotal moment where the path diverged, and choices echoed through the corridors of time. Melvin and I, at the nexus of our shared history, faced the consequences of decisions made and the uncertainties that loomed on the horizon.

As our life unfolded, the fragility of loyalty became apparent. Melvin, my steadfast companion, was not impervious to the allure of wandering affections. Yet, in the ebb and flow of our relationship, I found solace in the understanding that life's journey is a mosaic of experiences, and not all brushstrokes are painted with the same hues.

We navigated the tumultuous seas of our emotions, and when fidelity waned, we chose the path of understanding over resentment. The decision to part ways was not a defeat but an acknowledgment of life's intricate dance, where partners sometimes step out of sync.

In the aftermath of our separation, life took us on divergent trajectories. Melvin and I, once entangled in the tapestry of love, now walked separate paths. However, the echoes of our shared past lingered, casting shadows that stretched across the landscapes of our individual stories.

As I forged ahead, embracing the challenges of a life reshaped by choices, I found a reservoir of resilience within. The crossroads became a crucible of self-discovery, teaching me that destiny is not always about staying on a predetermined course but about adapting to the unforeseen turns.

Melvin, too, embarked on a journey of introspection. The fragments of our love story lingered in his heart, a testament to the indelible mark left by our time together. His path led him to confront the complexities of his own emotions, and in the crucible of change, he discovered facets of himself that had long been obscured.

The crossroads, it seemed, had not just been a moment of divergence but a catalyst for transformation. Our stories, once intertwined, evolved into narratives of individual growth and revelation. Destiny, in its enigmatic wisdom, guided us towards new beginnings, each step laden with the promise of healing and renewal.

As the chapter of "Crossroads of Destiny" unfolded, it became a poignant exploration of the impermanence of love, the resilience of the human spirit, and the profound impact of choices on the intricate tapestry of our lives.

# Chapter 10: Lost in Time

As I sit here, reminiscing about the chapters of my life, one thread stands out prominently—the bond I share with my children. Melvin, the father who stumbled through the labyrinth of love and parenthood, found solace and purpose in the laughter, tears, and tender moments with his kids.

Our home resonated with the echoes of joy when they arrived—the pitter-patter of tiny feet, the infectious laughter that could melt the coldest heart, and the countless bedtime stories that wove dreams around us. Melvin, in those moments, transformed into a storyteller, a protector, and above all, a loving father.

My children became the embodiment of hope and innocence. Each day was a new adventure, a canvas waiting to be painted with the vibrant hues of their laughter and endless curiosity. From teaching them to ride bicycles to wiping away tears after scraped knees, every experience forged an unbreakable connection between us.

Melvin's role extended beyond the conventional norms of fatherhood. He wasn't just a provider but a playmate, a confidant, and a guide navigating the uncharted waters of their young lives. The hours spent building forts in the living room, the bedtime rituals of tucking them in with tales of whimsical worlds, and the shared glances that spoke volumes—all of these moments defined the contours of our family's love.

The beauty of Melvin's love lay in its simplicity. He cherished the mundane as much as the extraordinary—a shared bowl of ice cream on lazy Sunday afternoons, impromptu dance parties in the living room, and the warmth of his embrace during thunderstorms that sent tremors through our little haven.

Parenthood, however, is not without its trials. Melvin faced each challenge with resilience, offering a steady hand and a reassuring smile. The lessons of life were imparted not through lectures but through the lived experiences we shared as a family. He became a beacon of strength, a source of unwavering support that anchored us in the stormy seas of life.

As the years passed, the dynamics shifted, and my children embarked on their journeys into the world. Melvin's love, however, transcended the constraints of time and distance. He became the silent cheerleader, the comforting voice on the other end of the phone, and the pillar of strength they could lean on.

In the tapestry of my life, the chapter titled "Lost in Time" is a celebration of the enduring love between a father and his children. Melvin's legacy is not just the shared DNA but the imprints of his love etched into the very fabric of their beings. The laughter, the tears, the shared dreams—all lost in time, yet forever embedded in the heartbeats of our shared journey.

# Chapter 11: Shattered Illusions

Life has a curious way of weaving unexpected threads into the fabric of our existence. In the midst of my own narrative, a chapter unfolded that not only challenged the boundaries of forgiveness but illuminated the profound capacity of the human heart to heal.

It all began with a somber revelation—Lena, now found herself entangled in the cruel clutches of illness. The news, delivered with a weight that echoed through my core, triggered a reflexive response within me. Despite the history of strained ties and the echoes of past grievances, an undeniable sense of empathy surged forth.

Without hesitation, I found myself at Lena's doorstep, determined to bridge the chasm that time and circumstance had carved between us. She was alone, grappling with the daunting shadows of her illness, and even her own son was absent. In that moment, it became apparent that compassion had to override the scars of the past.

Taking on the role of a caregiver was an unexpected turn, yet it felt strangely right. As I tended to Lena's needs, the silence between us spoke volumes. There were no words of apology, no grand gestures of reconciliation, just a shared understanding that transcended the spoken language. Lena, in her vulnerability, allowed me into the fortress of her solitude.

Days turned into weeks, and the routine of caregiving forged an unspoken alliance. Forgiveness, a balm for wounds deep-rooted, began to permeate the atmosphere. I forgave Lena not because she asked for it, but because I saw the genuine remorse in her eyes. Life had dealt her a challenging hand, and in those frail moments, illusions shattered, revealing the raw authenticity beneath.

Lena's acknowledgment of her past mistakes lingered in the air, unspoken yet palpable. There was a silent reconciliation, an unspoken pact that allowed healing to seep through the fractures of our shared history. As the sun dipped below the horizon, casting long shadows that mirrored the complexities of our relationship, a newfound understanding blossomed.

When Lena's journey reached its inevitable conclusion, the room held a serene calmness that transcended the grief. In those final moments, our connection had transcended the limitations of resentment. Lena departed with a sense of peace, and I, the unexpected caregiver, stood as a witness to the transformative power of forgiveness.

The chapter titled "Shattered Illusions" etched itself into the annals of my life as a testament to the resilience of the human spirit and the redemptive nature of compassion. In the ebb and flow of life, Lena and I found a fleeting yet profound connection, proving that even the most fractured bonds can be mended when draped in the cloak of understanding and forgiveness.

In the aftermath of Lena's passing, an unexpected tranquility settled upon me. The echoes of our shared history, once marred by resentment and hurt, now resonated with a profound sense of closure. Lena's departure became a poignant reminder of the transient nature of life and the importance of seizing opportunities for healing.

As I navigated the aftermath, I found solace in the knowledge that in Lena's final days, our relationship had undergone a metamorphosis. The burdens of past grievances had been lifted, and what remained were the fragments of a connection reborn in the crucible of vulnerability and forgiveness.

The funeral became a somber yet strangely serene affair. Lena's son, burdened with regret, found solace in the unspoken understanding that had evolved between his mother and me. In the absence of judgment, forgiveness had become the bridge spanning the gaps of our shared history.

As I stood by Lena's graveside, a myriad of emotions surged within me. Grief mingled with a sense of closure, and a quiet acknowledgment of the intricate dance that had unfolded between us. The headstone, a marker of finality, also bore witness to the unexpected beauty that emerged when two souls, once estranged, found a semblance of peace.

In the weeks that followed, memories of Lena lingered like soft whispers in the corridors of my mind. The role I had assumed as her caregiver became a defining moment, a testament to the resilience of the human spirit and the transformative power of forgiveness.

Lena's passing left behind a legacy—a lesson in embracing the imperfections of human connections and the possibility of redemption even in the eleventh hour. Our journey, marked by shattered illusions and eventual healing, served as a reminder that life's tapestry is woven with threads of both darkness and light.

As time unfolded, the chapter titled "Shattered Illusions" became a beacon of hope, illustrating that even in the face of life's complexities, compassion has the potential to bridge the divides that seem insurmountable. Lena's memory, once tinged with bitterness, evolved into a source of reflection on the fragile beauty of human connections and the capacity for growth and understanding, even in the face of life's inevitable partings.

# Chapter 12: Waves of Redemption

In the intricate tapestry of my own life, the twelfth chapter unfurls as a testament to the tumultuous journey I've traversed—marked by trials, tribulations, and an unwavering faith that weathered the storms. It's a narrative of resilience, forgiveness, and the unyielding hope I anchored in the Lord, even when faced with the darkest corners of human nature.

Life, with its capricious whims, hurled challenges my way, weaving a narrative that bore the scars of battles fought in the shadows. Amidst the struggles, I encountered a formidable adversary—someone who sought to exploit vulnerability, someone who tried to cast shadows over the light that flickered within.

The wounds inflicted were not just physical; they penetrated the very core of my spirit. But in the crucible of adversity, I discovered an inner strength that refused to be extinguished. The journey from victim to survivor was arduous, marked by tears shed in silence and battles waged in the recesses of my soul.

Amidst the darkness, the flicker of faith became my guiding light. The Lord, in His infinite wisdom, became my refuge, offering solace in moments of despair and whispering hope when the night seemed interminable. The journey, though arduous, was also a pilgrimage towards self-discovery and the realization that the Lord's grace could illuminate even the darkest corners.

As I emerged from the shadows, a pivotal moment awaited—forgiveness. The one who had sought to shatter my spirit, to break me down, was confronted not with vengeance, but with a resolute spirit fueled by the transformative power of forgiveness. It was not an act of forgetfulness but a conscious decision to unburden my heart from the weight of hatred.

The redemptive waves of forgiveness surged through my being, washing away the residue of pain. It was a testament to the strength drawn from my faith, a strength that allowed me to transcend the role of victim and embrace the mantle of a survivor.

The journey through the twelfth chapter was not without its moments of doubt and despair, but it became a testament to the resilience of the human spirit when anchored in unwavering faith. The scars remained, etched into the fabric of my existence, but they were now symbols of triumph rather than defeat.

As I stand at the precipice of this chapter, gazing back at the tumultuous seas I've navigated, I carry with me the lessons learned and the unwavering hope that even in the face of adversity, redemption is possible. The waves of redemption, though born from the depths of despair, carry me forward with a renewed sense of purpose—a purpose anchored in faith, forgiveness, and an unshakable belief in the Lord's guiding hand. Chapter 12: Waves of Redemption (Continued)

The waves of redemption, once set in motion, continued to shape the contours of my journey. The scars of the past, instead of being shackles, became markers of strength—a testament to the resilience that blossomed in the wake of adversity.

The process of forgiveness, though liberating, did not erase the memories. Rather, it transformed them into stepping stones towards a higher ground of healing. The one who had attempted to break me found no satisfaction in my harbored resentment. In forgiving, I reclaimed agency over my own narrative, severing the chains that tethered me to the shadows of the past.

As the redemptive waves reached their crescendo, I found solace not just in my own triumph but in the unwavering faith that had sustained me through the tempest. The Lord, my eternal refuge, remained the cornerstone of my strength. It was in the darkest moments that His light shone brightest, guiding me through the labyrinth of pain towards the shores of redemption.

The journey, though fraught with trials, had bestowed upon me a profound wisdom. I learned that forgiveness was not a concession to the wrongdoer but a gift to myself—an act of self-love that unshackled my spirit from the burdens of hatred. It was a testament to the transformative power of grace, a force that transcended the limitations of human understanding.

In the wake of forgiveness, a new chapter unfolded—one defined by healing, growth, and an unyielding hope for the future. The wounds, once festering, now bore witness to the miracle of renewal. The scars, far from being blemishes, became insignias of triumph—a living proof that the human spirit, fortified by faith and forgiveness, could rise from the ashes of despair.

As I emerged from the tumultuous waters of this chapter, I carried with me not just the echoes of past pain but the resonant hymn of redemption. The waves that once threatened to engulf me now propelled me forward, towards a horizon painted with the hues of possibility. In the symphony of my life, the twelfth chapter became a melodic ode to resilience, faith, and the enduring power of redemption.

Chapter 12: Waves of Redemption (Continued)

In the aftermath of forgiveness and the healing balm of redemption, a newfound sense of purpose and clarity illuminated my path. The scars that adorned my spirit were no longer reminders of weakness, but rather badges of courage and resilience that testified to the transformative journey I had traversed.

The waves of redemption, like a gentle current, carried me towards a future unburdened by the shadows of the past. My faith, unwavering despite the trials, became the compass guiding me forward. In the quiet moments of reflection, I found solace in the belief that the Lord, in His boundless mercy, had orchestrated the symphony of redemption in the midst of life's cacophony.

As I moved beyond the confines of victimhood, I became a beacon of hope for others navigating similar tempests. The scars, once concealed in shame, became a source of inspiration—a testament to the potency of resilience and the transformative power of forgiveness.

The one who sought to exploit my vulnerability inadvertently became a catalyst for my evolution. In embracing forgiveness, I not only severed the chains that bound me to the past but also extended a lifeline of compassion to the one who had attempted to dim the light within. It was a demonstration that even in the face of malevolence, the human spirit has the capacity to transcend, forgive, and rise anew.

The redemptive waves, having sculpted the landscape of my inner world, echoed with the whispers of hope and the promise of a future unbridled by the scars of yesterday. Life, once a turbulent sea, now revealed its gentler currents, guiding me towards serene shores where the echoes of pain faded into the background.

In this continued chapter of redemption, I discovered a reservoir of strength within myself—a strength drawn from the deep wells of faith, forgiveness, and an unwavering belief in the transformative power of love. As I embraced the dawn of a new day, I carried with me the lessons learned from the turbulent seas and stood on the precipice of tomorrow with an open heart, ready to embrace the limitless possibilities that lay ahead.

## Conclusion:

As I stand here on the precipice of tomorrow, the culmination of my journey, I can feel the weight of every step that led me to this moment. The whispers in the wind, the shattered reflections, and the echoes of silence now converge into a symphony of self-discovery.

Grief was once a torrential storm that threatened to engulf me, a force that seemed insurmountable. The whispers in the wind carried tales of resilience, reminding me that storms eventually yield to calm. In the quiet corners of my heart, I found solace in those whispers, and slowly, the tempest began to wane.

The shattered reflections were pieces of a broken reality, fragments of a life that once was. Each shard bore the scars of loss, and in navigating through the broken pieces, I discovered the art of rebuilding. It wasn't about recreating the past but crafting a new mosaic, one that bore the beauty of resilience.

Silence became both a sanctuary and a battleground. In the echoes of solitude, I confronted the void left by what once defined me. It was in the silence that I found the strength to face my own reflection, unmasked and vulnerable. The echoes guided me through the labyrinth of self-discovery, leading to the revelation that solitude could be a companion rather than an adversary.

Now, in this final chapter, I find myself at the threshold of a new dawn—a tapestry of tomorrow woven with threads of perseverance and hope. The struggles that once seemed insurmountable have become stepping stones toward a profound understanding of my own strength.

Life's harshness, faced with unwavering determination, has not extinguished the flame within me but has only made it burn brighter. The scars that mark my journey are not wounds to be hidden but badges of honor, each telling a story of resilience, courage, and growth.

I invite you, dear reader, to share in this moment of reflection. As the story concludes, I extend a hand to you, a fellow traveler in the journey of life. The tapestry of tomorrow is not just my own; it is a collective masterpiece woven by every soul that perseveres, believes, and emerges stronger.

The echoes of tranquility resonate in these closing lines, not as a distant melody but as a reminder that within each of us lies the power to weather life's storms. As this chapter closes, I hope you find inspiration to embark on your own journey of self-discovery, for in every ending, a new beginning awaits.

As I reflect on the intricate threads of my journey, I find myself at a crossroads where the past converges with the possibilities of the future. The symphony of self-discovery plays on, resonating with the sweet melody of lessons learned and the harmonious chords of resilience. In this moment of introspection, I realize that the tapestry of tomorrow is not just a destination but an ongoing creation, shaped by each deliberate step and every unexpected turn.

The struggles that marked my path were not mere obstacles; they were transformative moments that sculpted my character. Each trial was a chisel, refining the raw material of my existence into a work of art. As I stand on the threshold of tomorrow, I carry the wisdom earned through tears, the strength forged in the fires of adversity, and the unwavering belief in my own capacity to endure.

Life's harshness, once a formidable adversary, transformed into a stern but benevolent teacher. The lessons were often stern, the tests unforgiving, yet they paved the way for growth. The storms that threatened to consume me ultimately revealed the resilience inherent in the human spirit. Like a phoenix rising from the ashes, I emerged from the crucible of challenges stronger, more compassionate, and intimately aware of the fragility of life.

The scars etched on the canvas of my being are not marks of weakness but testimonials of battles fought and won. They are reminders that healing is a continuous process, and each scar tells a story of survival. I wear them proudly, for they symbolize the courage to confront pain and the ability to transform it into strength.

As the sun sets on this chapter, it casts long shadows that serve as reminders of the struggles overcome. Yet, in the fading light, there is a warm glow—a promise of a new dawn. The tapestry of tomorrow is woven with threads of hope, resilience, and the belief that, no matter how dark the night, there is always a dawn waiting to break.

In closing, I extend my gratitude to every character, every challenge, and every moment that contributed to the narrative of my life. To you, dear reader, who traversed these pages with me, I thank you for being a part of this shared journey. As the final lines unfold, I step into the unknown of tomorrow with a heart full of gratitude, a spirit fortified by resilience, and the unwavering belief that the best chapters are yet to be written.

## Note: A Message to the World

In the vast tapestry of life, I extend a humble note to the world—a testament forged from the crucible of my own experiences, a narrative woven with threads of faith, resilience, and the enduring power of hope.

The title note is a clarion call, urging each soul to be unwavering in their faith and to grasp onto hope with unyielding determination. Life, with its myriad challenges, may attempt to cast shadows upon our journey, but it is in these very shadows that the light of faith shines brightest.

In the labyrinth of trials, never underestimate the strength that lies within. Embrace faith as an anchor, grounding you amidst the storms that may assail. Hold steadfast to the belief that even in the darkest moments, a glimmer of hope can be found—a beacon guiding you towards the shores of redemption.

Seek the help you need, for there is no shame in acknowledging vulnerability. In reaching out, you not only extend a lifeline to yourself but create a network of support that can uplift those around you. Life's burdens are not meant to be borne alone, and asking for help is a testament to strength, not weakness.

As the author of this note, I implore you to cultivate a resilient spirit—one that rises from the ashes of adversity, strengthened by the fires of life's trials. The title note resonates with the echoes of my own journey, a journey marked by challenges that, through faith and hope, transformed into stepping stones towards a brighter tomorrow.

Let this note be a reminder to the world: in the symphony of life, let faith be your melody, let hope be your anthem, and let the echoes of resilience be the verses that narrate your story. For in the embrace of these virtues, we find the strength to overcome, the courage to endure, and the wisdom to navigate the ever-unfolding chapters of our lives.

**Thank you**

Made in the USA
Columbia, SC
04 April 2024